THETA
HEALING™

THETA HEALING™

Introducing an
Extraordinary Energy
Healing Modality

Vianna Stibal

HAY HOUSE, INC.

Carlsbad, California • New York City
London • Sydney • Johannesburg
Vancouver • Hong Kong • New Delhi

This book is dedicated:

To my God, the Creator of All That Is. It was under divine direction that the information contained in this book was received.

To my mother, who taught me to pray and to believe that God always hears and answers our prayers.

To my husband, who compiled the writing for this book, and who assisted me during my travels as I taught these techniques to the world. He is appreciated so much more than I could ever express.

To my children, who inspire me, who are my friends and who are all gifted intuitives.

To my precious grandchildren, who have brought blessings and joy into my life.

To all the ThetaHealing instructors and practitioners and the magnificent people throughout the world who have brought it to life. These wonderful people have been a source of joy to me. They are an inspiration to me on my journeys as I present these important techniques and concepts to the world.

And to those I have yet to meet, may your paths lead you to the place of greatest peace and abundant goodness.

❖❖❖❖❖

From the Editor: To our readers in the U.S. and Canada, please note that for the most part, we have maintained the British style of spelling, grammar (including noun/pronoun agreement), punctuation, and syntax of the most recent printing of this book, which was published in the United Kingdom.

Believe nothing,
No matter where you read it,
Or who has said it,
Not even if I have said it,
Unless it agrees with your own reason,
And your common sense.

Buddha

CONTENTS

PREFACE

In this book I will reveal one of the most powerful energy-healing techniques that has ever been written down: ThetaHealing™. ThetaHealing is a meditational process that brings about physical, psychological and spiritual healing with focused prayer through the Creator. The Creator has freely given us the fascinating knowledge you are about to receive. It has changed my life and the lives of many others.

There is one requirement that is absolute with this technique: you must have a central belief in the Creator of All That Is. I realize that the Creator has many different names; and God, Buddha, Shiva, Goddess, Jesus, Yahweh and Allah are all currents leading in a flow towards the Seventh Plane of Existence and the Creative Energy of All That Is. ThetaHealing has no religious affiliation. Neither are its processes specific to any age, sex, race, colour, creed or religion. Anyone with a pure belief in God or the Creative Force can access and use the branches of the ThetaHealing tree.

This book is a fusion of the past works of *Go Up and Seek God*, *Go Up and Work with God* and *The DNA 2 Advanced Manual*, with additional information developed since these works were written.

Even though I am sharing this information with you, I do not accept any responsibility for the changes that can occur from its use. The responsibility is yours, a responsibility you assume when you realize that you have the power to change your life as well as the lives of others through permission.

Please note, the remedies, approaches and techniques described herein are not meant to supplement, or be a substitute for, professional medical care or treatment. You should not treat a serious medical ailment without prior consultation from a qualified healthcare professional.

1

THE FORMATION OF THETAHEALING™

From the conception of the Orian Technique in 1994 to what ThetaHealing™ has become in the present day has been quite a journey. This journey has been shared with the wonderful ThetaHealing practitioners and instructors who support the work. ThetaHealing continues to grow as a beautiful tree in spring, watered by the interest of people around the world.

❖❖❖❖❖

My name is Vianna. I am the founder of what has become ThetaHealing. I was born with an inherent intuitive ability, although it was not my original plan to use this ability for healing. I began an initial study of Taoism, nutrition and herbs because of personal health problems. These interests eventually led me along the path to Nature's Path, which is the name of my business.

This path originally began in 1990, when I divorced my husband of ten years and had three young children to raise. I had heard that the government was required to hire a certain number of women for the Department of Energy. There was a Department of Energy facility relatively close to where I lived in Idaho Falls, Idaho. My plan was to work at what was called the 'Site' in nuclear security and still pursue my true interest in art. I knew that the bus ride to work would be long, but I thought the pay and benefits would be worth the effort.

It was in 1991 that I began the year-long training for the job of nuclear security guard. Competition was fierce and I had to learn skills that pushed me to the limit. After completing my training I took a job at a nearby manufacturing plant while I waited for my security clearance to work for the government.

During this time I never forgot my other interests. On breaks I would draw sketches of the other employees and give them short intuitive readings. This was shift work and I would often work from midnight to morning.

As a single mother, I soon realized that working as a security guard at a manufacturing plant did not offer the future that I wanted for my family. I knew that something had to change.

Health problems provided the incentive I needed to concentrate on the study of naturopathic medicine. Once I had finished the course in naturopathic medicine, in March 1994 I opened a business offering full-time massage, nutritional counselling and a naturopathic practice.

I came to the realization that I was following my life's path when doors began to open. I met a psychic who suggested that I do readings for income. As if by magic I had an office to work in, and from the very first day I always had clients to see. Within the first week I had met the person who was to become my best friend and had established repeat clients for readings. It was during these readings that I found that if I would listen, the voice of the Creator would give me instructions. I became quite good at the readings and was asked to do classes on the technique I was using. This was my beginning as a medical intuitive. From this time forward my metaphysical experiences increased exponentially to quantify who I was to become.

Meanwhile, I had developed a severe problem with my right leg. It would intermittently swell up to twice its normal size. Due to the inflammation and severe pain, I decided it was wise to seek conventional medical help. In the August of 1995, I was diagnosed with bone cancer. I was told that I had a tumour in my right femur. Every test that was performed at this time confirmed it. The bone specialist told me that he had seen only two other cases like mine. He also informed me that he felt amputation might be my best option. This, he said, would give me a little more time to live.

I felt as though darkness was gathering about me, and my ordeal was not over yet. My doctor sent me to the University of Utah for a biopsy. I was told that the procedure required my leg to be opened to allow the doctor to go in and take a bone sample by scraping the inside of my femur. I had no choice but to travel for four hours, in excruciating pain, for this biopsy. Blake, my husband at the time, drove me to Utah and I was admitted to the hospital. It was necessary for me to be awake for the procedure, forced to listen to the sounds of the hammer and drill. I was advised to stay in the hospital overnight, but Blake told the hospital staff that we were leaving because we had no insurance. I was too weak to argue with him. So, in incredible pain, I was bustled to the car and taken to spend the night at Blake's brother's house before the long drive home.

As I was leaving the hospital, I was told by the doctors that if I walked on my leg it would break. If this happened there would be no alternative but to amputate it to prevent the spread of the cancer. I was also informed that I might only have a couple of months to live anyway.

This ordeal put me on crutches for six weeks. I was still in unbearable pain from the tumour. My life seemed to be falling apart. I hobbled around on the crutches, living with constant pain and doubt as to how much longer I could actually survive. Still I went forward, continuing to see clients, not because of great courage or endurance, but because I had financial obligations and my young children needed me. Even though I was newly married to Blake, the relationship was anything but a true partnership and was an added burden on my declining health. I couldn't just give up and die, leaving my children alone. The very thought of them being sent to relatives, even to their father (who was paraplegic and ill), was unbearable. These thoughts gave me the will to live.

Even though I was very ill, my intuitive abilities became even more accurate, as did my connection to the Creator. All my life I had believed that I had a higher purpose from a promise that I made when I was 17. Now I was uncertain if I would complete it.

In confusion and sadness I sent forth a cry to the Creator: 'Why me? Why am I losing my leg? God, am I going to die? I have so much left to do!'

In the middle of this plea I heard a voice, as loud and clear as if the speaker was standing right next to me in the room: 'Vianna, you are here with or without a leg, so deal with it.'

I was astonished by this answer, but, although I didn't know it at the time, it was just what I needed. In that instant I became even more determined to find a way to heal my body.

Healers from the area where I lived heard of my plight, and people came from seemingly everywhere to help me. Some were wonderful healers, which I am sure kept me going through the dark times. The prayers that were made on my behalf kept me alive. I still thank God for Alice and Barbara helping to take away the pain.

I was a pitiful sight, hobbling into my office, leaning on my massage table to do massages and painfully struggling through readings. Adding to my problems, I had developed a staph infection in my leg. I decided that *enough was enough!* I was going to treat myself.

First, let me say that I have never been against conventional medicine. I believe that we should respect the opinions of trained healthcare professionals and in most cases they are likely to be correct. Even so, I felt that in my isolated case, the doctors were wrong in their diagnosis of bone cancer.

I trusted my intuition and the information I was receiving from the Creator and I began putting my knowledge of naturopathy to good use. I realized that it was vital for me to focus on aggressively cleaning out my body. I began a series of lemon cleanses as well as sauna cleanses. I spent a great deal of time in the sauna – four hours a day for over two and a half weeks. I took vitamins and minerals and I prayed constantly. Through it all, I still believed the medical diagnosis that the doctors had given me was wrong, but in spite of everything I was doing to help myself, I remained very sick.

My biopsy result finally came back and the result was negative for bone cancer, which confused the doctors, since every test performed earlier had shown a tumour. The biopsy had, however, revealed dead cells along with normal bone cells. The test result was sent to the Mayo Clinic, where they determined that I had lymphatic cancer that had killed the cells in my femur. I knew this to be the truth and I believed mercury poisoning had caused it. How? I knew this because I had gone up and asked God (or the Creator) and had received the message that I had been poisoned by mercury.

I began to search for answers as to how to get the mercury out of my system. I continued with cleanses, always trusting in the information that I received from the Creator. By this time my leg had physically shrunk and I was told by the doctors that in the event that I did survive, I would need physical therapy to enable me to walk correctly again.

I believed to the core of my being that God could heal in an instant, and in spite of everything that was happening, I continued to trust my intuition. Somehow I felt that I already knew how to heal myself. There was just something I was missing. I had used conventional medicine, cleanses, nutrition, oils, vitamins, affirmations and visualizations, and still I was sick. Every time I asked the Creator, I was told that I already knew the answer and that I just had to remember how to call upon God.

The answer to my prayers came while I was in the mountains. I held a gathering with some friends where we camped out and shared a pot luck dinner. Each person that came brought a dish for the gathering. My aunt from Oregon showed up unexpectedly, but had a bad stomachache. She lay down in a tent and I went inside to help her. She knew that I was a naturopath, but I had no herbs with me. The intense pain that she was in led me to believe that it might be her appendix. I began to do a body scan, as I had done with others hundreds of times before. I went out of the top of my head, through my crown chakra, as I would do when giving a reading, and when I was in my aunt's space I asked the Creator what was the matter with her and I was shown that it was giardia. I told it to go away and witnessed the Creator releasing the pain in her stomach. Within seconds, it had gone. She was able to get up and felt much better. This incident gave me food for thought and encouraged me to use it again.

The next day a man came into my practice with a severe backache. Reflecting on what had happened with my aunt, I did the same procedure on him. Instantly, his back pain was gone.

That night, I pondered over the events of the past days. I decided it was time to do the same thing to myself.

The following day I hobbled into my office, excited at the prospect of carrying out the same procedure on my leg. I thought to myself, 'It can't be this easy!'

I stopped just before the door to my office and went out of my space from my crown chakra and prayed to the Creator. I then commanded a healing on myself, and it worked! My right leg, which had shrunk to three inches shorter than my left leg, returned instantly to its normal size. The pain was removed and my leg was healed.

I was so incredibly excited about my healing that throughout the day I compulsively tested the strength in my newly healed leg, curious to see if the pain would return.

Today my femur continues to be healthy, all test reports are normal and I am free of lymphatic cancer. In my gratitude I made a vow to the Creator to give this technique to all those who wanted to learn it. This was the foundation of the ThetaHealing that we know and love today.

Interestingly, I still have the x-rays of my leg. A few years ago, they were taken to a bone specialist for a second opinion, and he pronounced that the owner of the leg must surely be dead!

The next person that I used the technique on was a little girl. A woman named Audrey Miller had a great-granddaughter with health difficulties and brought the child to me to be healed. She knew nothing about the instantaneous healing to my leg.

I asked her, 'Why did you bring her to me?'

Audrey looked at me with her soulful eyes and said, 'God told me to bring her to you.'

I remember how she walked up to me and placed the child in my arms. The child's own arms were tiny; she had gained no weight at all in the past two years. She had been born with her legs out of their sockets and she had a heart murmur. She also had what I can only term 'a bad attitude'.

I knew that I had been healed, so I told Audrey that it would take six days to heal the child, thinking that this would be plenty of time. I was excited about this new technique, but also very anxious. I remember crying to the Creator, 'Oh, dear Lord, please help me heal this child. Please, God, please, heal this child.' Then I went up to use the procedure I had been shown.

Each day for six days, Audrey's daughter drove for two hours to bring the child to me to be worked on for half an hour. I put her under coloured lights and used the new healing technique.

The little girl was using crutches to walk, the kind that attached to her arms. On the third day, she stood up and told me that she could walk and that she was going to walk to her grandmother without crutches. I said to her, 'Oh no, honey, you can't do that yet. You aren't strong enough.' But, stubbornly, she told me that she was going to do it. She stood up and walked about three or four feet to her grandmother. That was the first time she had ever walked on her own. I was totally amazed!

After that I watched her back straighten out and she expelled several tapeworms. Her heart murmur had now gone and she started, with physical therapy, to learn how to walk properly. Now that she had the strength, she could teach her body to walk without assistance. The most amazing part of this healing was that she gained two pounds in just three days, and in six days, she had gained four pounds.

Something was working! Excited, I began to use the technique on everyone. I treated all kinds of different diseases and infirmities and started working with people who were terminally ill. People from all walks of life found me by word of mouth. I found that the healings were extremely successful with clients that I already had, and soon new clients were coming from all over the world. Many of them were healed instantly, while others took a few sessions, and others simply did not heal.

After using the procedure with varying degrees of success, I came to a conclusion about why this technique was working so well. I came to believe that we were doing these healings from a 'Theta state' of mind. I had some knowledge of Theta because my by then former husband Blake was a hypnotist. He had many books about the subconscious mind and I had occasionally read these books. My theory was that we were going into the Theta state to bring about these healings. If my theory was correct, then I had a breakthrough in healing and an explanation of faith healing that could be scientifically measured.

2

THE FORMATION OF CLASSES

I knew that Theta was not a new theory of healing. Many hypnotists had actually worked with people in the Theta state. They had brought the client and also the health practitioner to a Theta state and achieved amazing results. I was also convinced that when you called upon God in this state, you could plug in, as if to an electrical socket, and actually heal a person instantly. I was already getting extremely good results, but I knew that it could be perfected if I had a better understanding of what I was doing, so I commenced investigating.

The human mind has five different brainwaves: Alpha, Beta, Gamma, Delta and Theta. These are constantly in motion; the brain is consistently producing waves in all of these frequencies. Everything that you do and everything you say is regulated by the frequency of your brainwaves.

A Theta state is a very deep state of relaxation, the state used in hypnosis. In Theta, the brainwaves are slowed to a frequency of four to seven cycles per second. Sages meditate for hours to reach this state, as in it they are able to access absolute calm. Theta brainwaves can be thought of as the subconscious; they govern the part of our mind that is layered between the conscious and the unconscious. They hold memories and sensations. They also govern our attitudes, beliefs and behaviour. They are always creative and inspirational and are characterized by very spiritual sensations. We believe this state allows us to act below the level of the conscious mind.

Theta is a very powerful state. It can be likened to the trance-like state that children attain when they are playing video games and are completely oblivious to what is going on around them. Another example of the use of the Theta state is that of the Tibetan priests. In winter, these priests place wet towels over their shoulders. Within minutes the towels are completely dry. In ancient times the Kahunas of Hawaii accessed the Theta state to walk on hot lava.

I began to teach this technique in the classes that I held locally. During my first class, a student stood up and told me that it was absolutely impossible to 'hold' a conscious Theta state. He said that he had been working with biofeedback for many years and unless a person was in a deep sleep hypnotic state, they just could not hold a Theta state. He claimed that the other brainwaves would interfere. He said that it was a great theory, but it was impossible. I was amused by his response and felt more determined than ever to prove my theory.

Validation for the Theta state came when a friend and student became interested in the work. He was a physicist who worked at the nuclear site outside town. He made us an electroencephalograph, and that's when things became interesting. In my classes, we hooked up people from all healing modalities to the machine. We found that people who were Reiki practitioners utilized the high Alpha brainwave. The Alpha brainwave is a wonderful healing wave. In fact, some Japanese scientists believe strongly in it because Alpha waves 'remove' pain and relax the body.

We confirmed that the technique we were using to do the healings was taking us to a Theta state. Every single person was going into Theta, even those just learning the technique. And we found that not only were the practitioners going into Theta, but the people they were working on were also going into Theta. We believed that the healings were taking place in a state of what I call 'God-consciousness'.

We continued to teach people as fast as we could. The classes were filled with wonderful people all eager to learn the technique. More and more people were learning and having a great time.

With continued practice, I found the healings became even more detailed and impressive. The results improved and my clientèle increased daily, but I still encountered a few people who would not heal.

One of those was a woman who had diabetes. Although her pain disappeared, her legs got better and so many other things improved for her, I could not keep her diabetes under control. Her blood sugar level still fluctuated dangerously. I knew that this type of diabetes was caused by a chromosome and I tried everything, even commanding the body to have its perfect blueprint. I was told that this did not work because the body thought it was perfect the way it was.

It was while working with this woman that I made a very interesting discovery. When I went 'up' and asked to see the chromosome that was causing her diabetes, in the rapture of Theta I was shown another chromosome that I was told was the chromosome of youth and vitality. Then I heard the voice of the Creator guiding me in a story of human DNA. I was told that this particular chromosome had been changed during the history of humankind's evolution. In a time and consciousness that is now lost to us, we were able to rejuvenate our body. We lost this ability over thousands of years, and because of this, this chromosome is now incomplete. However, in this time of enlightenment we are once again ready to receive regenerated youth.

I was told that the lost keys of youth and vitality in the DNA code were going to be vital to human survival in the years to come. This was, in part, because of the poisons and toxins that we would be subjected to in the modern industrial age. I was told that as a larger degree of the population became intuitive, they would become more sensitive to the physical world, but the completion of the youth and vitality chromosome would help them survive.

I was so excited about the new discovery that I forgot all about the chromosome for diabetes. I gave the woman with diabetes a hug, told her that I would work with her the next day and sent her home.

At the time, I was sharing my office with my friends Kevin and Chrissie. With glowing enthusiasm I told them all about what I had seen. I also told them that I had been given instruction on how to work on the chromosome and how to complete it. They were fascinated by the concepts and listened intently as I told them the process. I activated myself first and then Kevin and Chrissie. That evening I was given more information and guidance. In the coming days I was repeatedly shown how to change the youth and vitality chromosome until the Creator was sure that I had understood the information. This was the beginning of the DNA activation (see Chapter 26).

The Creator told me to begin with the DNA activation, activating the phantom DNA strands in a person's body. Understand that in this process we are not actually adding strands to anyone, we are only awakening what is already there. I was told that through this activation a person's intuition is improved, their ability to heal is improved, their body detoxifies and they are able to access the different planes of existence effortlessly. When I activated myself, I found that my 'laughter lines' began to fade away and my body started rejuvenating. I felt younger.

It was at this time that I hosted a radio talk show. I scheduled myself to speak about the Theta technique. When the radio staff asked me what it was called, I told them that I had always called it ThetaHealing. They advised me to choose another name because they felt that the name sounded like Scientology.

I told Kevin and Chrissie about this and we all sat down to brainstorm an alternate name. I remember us sitting on the floor of the office, laughing in our bare feet. I can still see Kevin with his long red hair and infectious laughter and Chrissie with her serious metaphysical demeanour. We remembered that the technique had been called many names. The first name I remembered was the Wilson technique, which was used for remote viewing in 1928. But we went even farther back in time and Kevin and I agreed upon the name 'Orian' (with an 'a'). This was the name that we used: the Orian technique.

For the first few years I continued with this name, but ThetaHealing was more to my liking. Today we use the name 'ThetaHealing' for the brainwave Theta, originating from the Egyptian and Greek letter *theta*, meaning, among other things, 'soul'. The Orian technique was originally associated with the DNA activation, but ThetaHealing represents the complete healing modality, which stems from the thousands of readings, not to mention hundreds of classes and seminars, that I have done. Today both the names – 'Orian technique' and 'ThetaHealing' – are used, but ThetaHealing has become mainstream.

From the time of the talk show ThetaHealing began to take on a living essence of its own. Then I received a message from the Creator. In spite of all that was happening in my personal life, the Creator told me to take this information to the world and to share it with others. I told the Creator that I was the wrong person to do this. In fact, I spent several hours discussing it with the Creator. I had actually already given my word to take it to the world, but now the true ramifications of this responsibility were hitting home.

I remember reasoning with the Creator. I said, 'Okay, if you want me to take this to the world, then send me a doctor, one who can tell me that this is the way a chromosome actually works, a doctor that will actually listen to me, a doctor who is open enough spiritually to listen to what I have to say. You also need to send me someone to write a book, because I am just too busy.'

I had many reasons for asking for all this. At that particular time in my life, my son's wife was pregnant and so was my daughter, and they were all living in my home. I was in the middle of a nasty divorce and I was taking care of all of these people by myself. I felt that my whole world was falling apart right before my eyes, and in the midst of all of this, I was being told by the Creator to take ThetaHealing to the world! I just couldn't understand how I could do any more than I was already doing.

So I was perplexed when the Creator said, 'You will write the book, Vianna.'

But I also knew that God never asks you to do anything without providing a way for you to do it.

Shortly thereafter, Audrey Miller came into my office quite unexpectedly and told me that I was going to the Universal Light Workers' Conference. I had seen the flyer for this and wanted to go, but I couldn't afford it.

But now this wonderful woman was willing to pay my fare and all of my expenses, including my food and everything else that I needed. She told me that I needed to meet a doctor who was speaking there. Apparently he was speaking about DNA. Audrey knew about the DNA activation that I was doing and thought that the two of us should meet. This was validation enough for me.

When it came near the time to go, however, I balked, because I didn't want to leave my children at such a difficult time in their lives. The more I thought about it, the worse I felt. I made myself sick with anxiety. I was torn between staying and going. Needless to say, by the time I got to the conference, I was feeling pretty wrung out.

The first person that I met at the conference was the doctor I had asked God to show me. At the time he was doing extensive work with lasers and DNA. He seemed to be open-minded, so I tentatively began to tell him about what I was visualizing in the DNA activation. As we talked, he told me the names and functions of everything that I was seeing in the chromosomes – the shadow chromosomes, the telomeres – and he not only validated what I was seeing but said it was unlikely that I could have known some of this without having been instructed in some way. I told him that this was what God had shown me, and that inside the brain was the 'central cell' (so called by my friend Kevin) that was located in the pineal gland. This 'master cell' (as the doctor called it) is the creation point for sending messages to the rest of the body

I apparently piqued the doctor's curiosity. After our meeting he called on me to remote-view clients as he visited them. He tested me with these people and asked me questions about what I could 'see' in their bodies. Then he not only confirmed what I had seen but his curiosity in my ability to 'see' what was going on in the body allowed me to know that I was viewing something real.

At the same conference I met Robert, who was a publisher. He had been involved with metaphysics before and as we talked he became interested in the DNA knowledge. We agreed that he should come to Idaho to transcribe the channelled material. I recorded the DNA activation technique for him and he and I agreed to co-author a small book. But when he took the recordings home to California, he wrote it and published it in pamphlet form, listing himself as the main author with my name in small print at the bottom. Much to my dismay, he changed the material so much and added so much filler that it had little to do with the original knowledge that I had given him. This book came out in 1997. This was a great disappointment to me and a betrayal of my trust; however, it encouraged me to rewrite the book and publish it myself.

By this time I felt that I could not trust anyone to compile a book on ThetaHealing, not even my closest friends. I decided to write the information down myself, in the form that it came to me from Creator, so that the vital points were not lost. God had once again worked in a strange way and I was guided by a divine plan. My first transcribed ThetaHealing book was called *Go Up and Seek God*.

True to my promise to the Creator, I began to teach classes throughout the United States in 1998. These were the first of the DNA 1 classes, where I taught the DNA activation and the early Orian Technique. In 1999, I created the first Teacher's Course to certify teachers in the Orian Technique. This was held at a place called Triple Creek in La Bell, Idaho. The course is now taught several times a year and I have been certifying teachers ever since. A *DNA 2 Teacher's Manual* was developed for it and is now updated constantly. The Creator was right; I would take the technique to the world.

I continued to see clients, and by the end of 1999 I had done over 20,000 readings and healings. As time went on I received more information and transcribed the book *Go Up and Work with God* in the year 2000. In this book, the belief work that came to me was put on paper for the first time. About this time, the DNA 1 Class (in what was then a two-day class) grew into what became known as DNA 2, a three-day class, in order to encompass the belief work. By the year 2000 I was teaching internationally.

One of the greatest things I have discovered while working on clients is that we hold the keys to our own health, our body and our vitality. The information I was given allows us to change our *beliefs*, and the systems that guide our decisions, in an instant. These are the beliefs and programmes we learned from childhood and from other aspects of our *being*. Some of them have been passed on from generation to generation.

In the following pages you will learn how to work on all four levels of all that you are: the *core belief level*, the *genetic level*, the *history level* and the *soul level*. It is through the removal and replacement of programmes on these four levels that the body is enabled to conquer physical illness and remove emotional blockage. This belief work will enable you to create the life that you want for yourself, for it is a truth that we create our own reality and that we are all connected to God. I am going to share with you the tools to change what you formerly believed, reverse the negative effect these beliefs have had on you and create the life you desire.

In the year 2000, a new class was shown to me called 'Psychic Anatomy'. I have since changed the name of this class to 'Intuitive Anatomy'. The first class was held at my old Channing Way, Idaho Falls, offices. It was designed to assist people to 'see' the inside of the body for healing, as an aid to the Theta technique. The body of knowledge of this class is held in the *Intuitive*